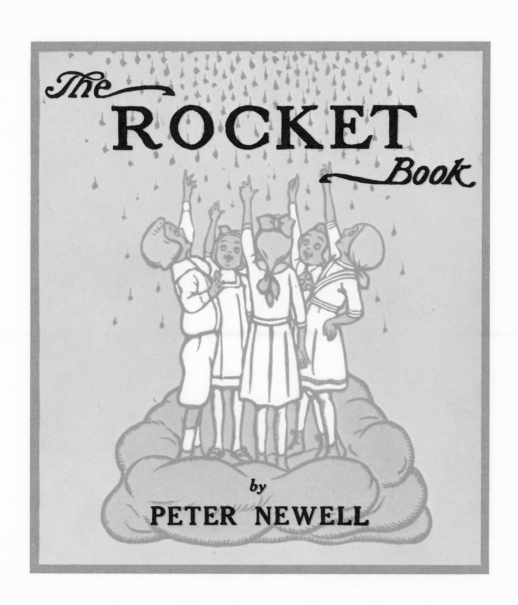

The ROCKET Book

by

PETER NEWELL

Dover Publications, Inc.
New York

Published in Canada by General Publishing Company, Ltd., 30 Lesmill Road, Don Mills, Toronto, Ontario.
Published in the United Kingdom by Constable and Company, Ltd., 10 Orange Street, London WC 2.

This Dover edition, first published in 1974, is an unabridged and unaltered republication of the work originally published in 1912. This book is reprinted by special arrangement with Harper & Row, publishers of the original edition.

International Standard Book Number: 0-486-22044-3
Library of Congress Catalog Card Number: 68-9155

Manufactured in the United States of America
Dover Publications, Inc.
180 Varick Street
New York, N. Y. 10014

THE ROCKET BOOK

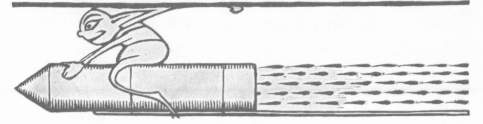

THE BASEMENT

When Fritz, the Janitor's bad kid,
   Went snooping in the basement,
He found a rocket snugly hid
   Beneath the window casement.

○

He struck a match with one fell swoop;
   Then, on the concrete kneeling,
He lit the rocket and—she—oop!
   It shot up through the ceiling.

FIRST FLAT

The Steiners on the floor above
  Of breakfast were partaking;
Crash! came the rocket, unannounced,
  And set them all a-quaking!

It smote a catsup bottle, fair,
  And bang! the thing exploded!
And now these people all declare
  That catsup flask was loaded.

SECOND FLAT

Before the fire old Grandpa Hopp
   Dozed in his arm-chair big,
When from a trunk the rocket burst
   And carried off his wig!

It passed so near his ancient head
   He roused up with a start,
And, turning to his grandsons, said,
   " You fellows think you're smart!"

THIRD FLAT

Algernon Bracket, somewhat rash,
   Had blown a monster bubble,
When, oh! there came a blinding flash,
   Precipitating trouble!

But Algy turned in mild disgust,
   And called to Mama Bracket,
" Say, did you hear that bubble bu'st?
   It made an awful racket!"

FOURTH FLAT

Jo Budd, who'd bought a potted plant,
    Was dousing it with water.
He fancied this would make it grow,
    And Joseph loved to potter.

●

Then through the pot the rocket shot
    And made the scene look sickly!
"Well, now," said Jo, "I never thought
    That plant would shoot so quickly!"

FIFTH FLAT

Right here 'tis needful to remark
　　That Dick and " Little Son "
Were playing with a Noah's ark
　　And having loads of fun,

When all at once that rocket, stout,
　　Up through the ark came blazing!
The animals were tossed about
　　And did some stunts amazing.

SIXTH FLAT

A Burglar on the next floor up
  The sideboard was exploring.
(The family, with the brindled pup,
  Were still asleep and snoring.)

●

Just then, up through the silverware
  The rocket thundered, flaring!
The Burglar got a dreadful scare;
  Then out the door went tearing.

SEVENTH FLAT

Miss Mamie Briggs with no mean skill
   Was playing " Casey's Fling "
To please her cousin, Amos Gill,
   Who liked that sort of thing,

●

When suddenly the rocket, hot,
   The old piano jumbled!
It stopped that rag-time like a shot,
   Then through the ceiling rumbled.

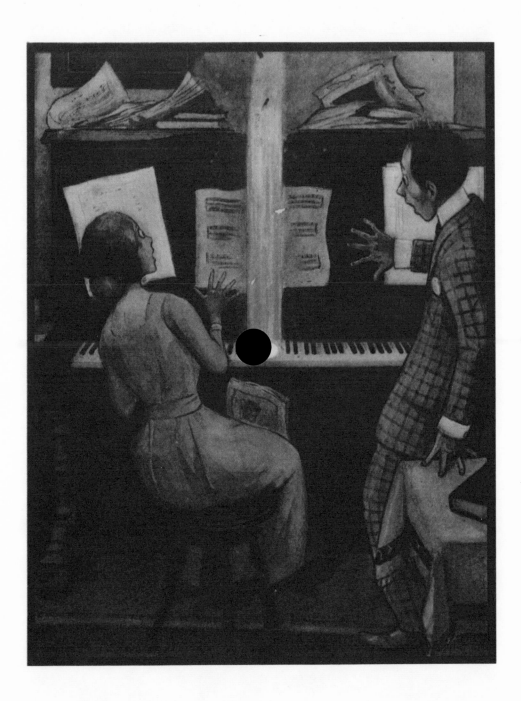

EIGHTH FLAT

Up through the next floor on its way
    That rocket, dread, went tearing
Where Winkle stood in bath-robe, gay,
    A tepid bath preparing.

●

The tub it punctured like a shot
    And made a mighty splashing.
The man was rooted to the spot;
    Then out the door went dashing.

NINTH FLAT

Bob Brooks was puffing very hard
  His football to inflate,
While round him stood his faithful guard,
  And they could hardly wait.

Then came the rocket, fierce and bright,
  And through the football rumbled.
" You've got a pair of lungs, all right!"
  His staring playmates grumbled.

TENTH FLAT

The family dog, with frenzied mien,
  Was chasing Fluff, the mouser,
When, poof! the rocket flashed between,
  And quite astonished Towzer.

●

Now, if this dog had wit enough
  The English tongue to torture,
He might have growled such silly stuff
  As, " Whew! that cat's a scorcher!"

ELEVENTH FLAT

While Carrie Cook sat with a book
  The phonograph played sweetly.
Then came the rocket and it smashed
  That instrument completely.

Fair Carrie promptly turned her head,
  Attracted by the roar.
" Dear me, I never heard," she said,
  " That record played before!"

TWELFTH FLAT

De Vere was searching for a match
  To light a cigarette,
But failed to find one with despatch,
  Which threw him in a pet.

Just then the rocket flared up bright
  Before his face and crackled,
Supplying him the needed light—
  " Thanks, awfully," he cackled.

THIRTEENTH FLAT

Home from the shop came Maud's new hat—
  A hat of monstrous size!
It almost filled the tiny flat
  Before her ravished eyes.

When, sch-u-u! up through the box so proud
  The rocket flared and spluttered.
" I said that hat was all too loud!"
  Her peevish husband muttered.

FOURTEENTH FLAT

Tom's pap had helped him start his train,
  And all would have been fine
Had not the rocket, raising Cain,
  Blocked traffic on the line.

It blew the engine into scrap,
  As in a fit of passion.
" Who would have thought that toy," said pap,
  " Would blow up in such fashion!"

FIFTEENTH FLAT

Orlando Pease, quite at his ease,
  The " Morning Star " was reading.
" My dear," said he to Mrs. Pease,
  " Here's a report worth heeding."

●

The rocket then in wanton sport
  Flashed through the printed pages.
The lady gasped, " A wild report!"
  Then swooned by easy stages.

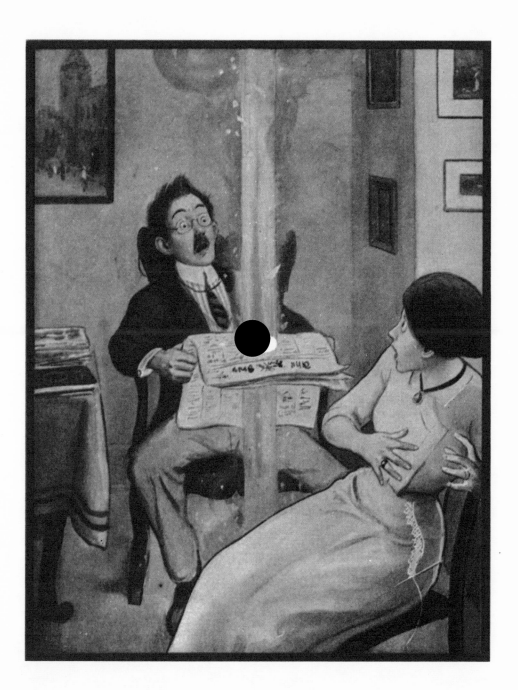

SIXTEENTH FLAT

Doc Danby was a stupid guy,
  So, lest he sleep too late,
He placed a tattoo clock near by
  To waken him at eight.

●

But, ah! the rocket smote that clock
  And smashed its way clean through it!
"You have a fine alarm," said Doc,
  "But, say, you overdo it!"

SEVENTEENTH FLAT

A penny-liner, Abram Stout,
   Was writing a description.
" The flame shot up," he pounded out—
   Then threw a mild conniption.

●

For through his Flemington there shied
   A rocket, hot and mystic.
" I didn't mean to be," he cried,
   " So deuced realistic!"

EIGHTEENTH FLAT

Gus Gummer long had set his head
  Upon some strange invention.
" Be careful, Gus," his good wife said;
  " It might explode. I mention—"

Just then the pesky rocket flared
  And wrecked that Yankee notion.
" I feared as much!" his wife declared;
  Then fainted from emotion.

NINETEENTH FLAT

While Burt was on his hobby-horse
  And riding it like mad,
The rocket on its fiery course
  Upset the startled lad.

The frightened pony plunged a lot,
  Like Fury playing tag.
"Whoa, Spot!" said Burt. "Who would have
    thought
  You such a fiery nag!"

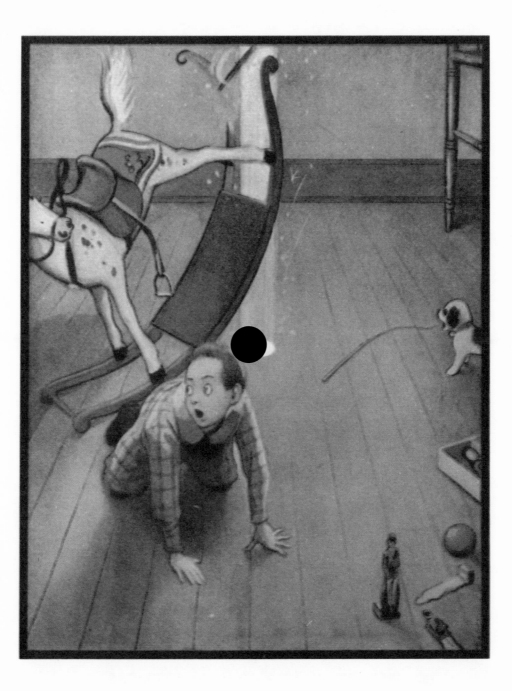

TWENTIETH FLAT

A taxidermist plied his trade
  Upon a walrus' head.
It really made him quite afraid
  To meet its stare so dread.

●

When suddenly the rocket, bright,
  Flared up and then was off!
" Oh, Minnie," cried the man in fright,
  " Just hear that walrus cough!"